D0462015

Grasses & Gravestones

Glen Sorestad

SmokyPeace

Smoky Peace Press

Grande Prairie, Alberta

An earlier version of "The Dozer Man and the Owl" was published in
Stalking Place: Poems Across Borders by Hawk Press, 1988, Hobbes,
New Mexico.

Smoky Peace Press
6425 96A Street
Grande Prairie, Alberta, Canada T8W 2B5
sdeimert@telusplanet.net

National Library of Canada Cataloguing in Publication Data

Sorestad, Glen A., 1937-
  Grasses & gravestones / Glen Sorestad.

  Poems.
  ISBN 0-9685623-3-7

  I. Title. II. Grasses and gravestones.
PS8587.O746G72 2003   C811'.54   C2003-910985-2

Acknowledgements

"The Dozer Man & The Owl" appeared in an earlier version in the volume, *Stalking Place: Poems Across Borders* (Hawk Press, New Mexico, 1988).

The author appreciates the editorial insights and constructive criticism of his wife Sonia in the final revisions of these poem sequences, and wishes to thank Elroy Deimert, as well, for his editorial suggestions and for his enthusiasm for this project.

Glen Sorestad

Glen Sorestad was born in Vancouver in 1937, but moved to the prairies when he was ten and grew up on a farm in east-central Saskatchewan, attending a one-roomed country school before they vanished from the scene. He later became a school teacher and taught for over 20 years, the last dozen years in a high school in Saskatoon. He earned a Master's Degree in Education with distinction from the University of Saskatchewan. He began writing seriously in 1968, co-founded Thistledown Press in 1975 with his wife Sonia, and quit teaching in 1981 to pursue his writing and publishing activities. He was president of Thistledown Press from 1975 to 2000 when he and his wife retired from literary publishing.

Over the years Sorestad's poetry and stories have been published across Canada, in the United States, in England, Scotland, Denmark, Finland, Norway and Slovenia. He has authored or co-authored fifteen books of poems and his poetry has been frequently broadcast on CBC radio, on radio stations in the United States, and on state public radio in Norway. His poetry has been translated into several languages including Spanish, Norwegian, Finnish and Slovenian. He is the editor or co-editor of many anthologies of poetry and stories, including most recently an international anthology, *Something to Declare*, by Oxford University Press and a poetry anthology, *In The Clear*, from Thistledown. His poems have appeared in over 40 different anthologies and textbooks, while his stories have also been anthologized; one of his stories was produced for television in Canada by Bravo TV.

Sorestad has given well over 300 readings of his work in every province of Canada and in 15 states, including Oregon, California, Arizona, New Mexico, Texas, Arkansas and Minnesota. He has also read his poetry in Strasbourg, France and at several places in Norway, including a literary salon in his honour at the Canadian Ambassador's residence in Oslo. Most recently he was a featured poet at two important international literary events: the 2001 Lahti International Writers Reunion in Finland, and again in Vilenica, 2002, in Slovenia. Over the years he has presented his poetry publicly in diverse venues: schools, colleges and universities, libraries, art galleries, bookstores, restaurants, coffee bistros, bars, community halls, churches, maritime museums, ski resorts, private clubs, and even in the Cowboy Hall of Fame in Lea County, New Mexico.

Sorestad was honoured with a Life Membership in the League of Canadian Poets. In November of 2000 he was appointed the first Poet Laureate of Saskatchewan, becoming the first provincially or federally appointed Poet Laureate in Canada. He was awarded the Saskatoon Book Award in November 2001 for *Leaving Holds Me Here*. In February 2003, he received the Queen's Golden Jubilee Medal for contributions to his country.

He and his wife, Sonia, live in Saskatoon. They have four adult children and ten grandchildren.

Books of Poetry by Glen Sorestad

Prairie Pub Poems (chapbook). Anak Press, Wood Mountain, 1973.

Wind Songs (chapbook). Thistledown Press, Saskatoon, 1975.

Prairie Pub Poems. Thistledown Press, Saskatoon, 1976.

Pear Seeds in My Mouth (chapbook). Sesame Press, Windsor, 1977.

Ancestral Dances. Thistledown Press, Saskatoon, 1979.

Jan Lake Poems. Harbour Publishing, Madeira Park, 1984.

Hold the Rain in Your Hands: Poems New & Selected. Coteau Books, Regina, 1985.

Stalking Place: Poems Across Borders. Hawk Press, New Mexico, 1988 (with Jim Harris & Peter Christensen).

Air Canada Owls. Nightwood Editions, Madeira Park, 1990.

West Into Night. Thistledown Press, Saskatoon, 1991.

Jan Lake Sharing (chapbook). Privately printed, Saskatoon, 1993 (with Jim Harris).

Birchbark Meditations (chapbook). Writers of the Plains, New Mexico, 1996.

Icons of Flesh. Ekstasis Editions, Victoria, 1998.

Today I Belong to Agnes. Ekstasis Editions, 2000.

Leaving Holds Me Here: Selected Poems 1975-2000. Thistledown Press, Saskatoon, 2001. (Saskatoon Book Award, 2001).

Dreaming My Grandfather's Dreams (chapbook). Frog Hollow Press, Victoria, 2002.

Grasses & Gravestones. Smoky Peace Press, Grande Prairie, 2003.

Contents

The Grass at Batoche

The Grass at Batoche

... for Clive Doucet
and John B. Lee

So many times now have I
walked this grass
as if for the first time,
strode across the battle scars,
the wounds of the past,
and always it is the same—
a now-familiar, inexplicable
pin-pricking of the senses,
a feeling something
elusive lies here
that begs understanding,
drawing me back.

I claim no Metis blood.
no roots of mine reach
back to when the people
of Batoche tried to claim
their place at the table
and were denied. Yet these names,
the acts chiselled in the cemetery markers
seem close as the simple epitaphs
marking my ancestral headstones
in that small country churchyard
several hundred miles east of here.

Dumont, Laframboise,
Ouellette, Letendre–
why do these names resound
as if they *were* my people,
as if part of my own history
could be heard in the whispers
of wind through prairie grass?

Two friends accompany me—
different geographies, different
family histories— one whose roots
spring from Acadian Cape Breton;
the other from Ontario farm folk.
Here, at this site, we three are
an essence of the nation's history:
Acadien, United Empire Loyalist,
clothed in the victories and defeats
of their own family histories, and I,
descendant of later arrivals lured
from Europe to the endless and lush
agoraphobic sea of prairie
grass and boundless sky.
East coast, central Canada,
and the west— each of us
bringing some unspoken desire
focussed for the moment on this grass
we swish, circling always
towards that private inner place
where each of us must go.

15

We move with deliberateness
through the ageless grass,
not snake-wary but as if
with each footfall we might
reopen history's many wounds,
our eyes and ears and hearts
alert to whatever lies before us
whatever the grasses may disclose,
alert to telltale signs, portents,
revelations, small epiphanies.

What we all want is
to wear this landscape
like a jacket when we leave,
just as we wear the places
we have come from or have been.
To do so we each must leave
some part of us behind
when we go.

Ole Sorestad claimed homestead
on the hunting territory of Crees
and believed he owned the land–

east-central Saskatchewan
twenty years after Riel was hanged
from a scaffold in Regina.

Family lore says Grandfather's
first encounter with the Crees
who had no homesteading rights

occurred when a tipi sprouted
one evening in the open pasture
a quarter-mile from the house.

After chores Grandfather set off
to discover who was camped
on land he thought of as his own.

Later to his family he reported
dark-skinned people sitting in a circle
"in a peechaboo eating lynch meat."

Next day tipi and occupants vanished
with morning mist. My grandfather
never went to Batoche, knew

little of its story. Less than
two hundred miles and twenty years distant,
it was a tale he hadn't been told.

I peel out of the car
a sultry August day,
about to enter Batoche
Interpretive Centre.

A grandfather and grandson
are just coming out.
We exchange greetings,
begin to chat, two grandfathers–
one a direct descendant
of a Metis defender killed
those fateful days in May, 1885.

He has brought his grandson
from a distant city
because he says
      it's very important
      for him to know who he is
      and where he's come from.

How could I disagree?
The rest of the day I imagine
 the maelstrom of emotions
and memories inside as he
walks with his grandson
through fields of history
where his ancestors were
dispossessed, scattered–
into another century,
a people without identity .

This is the history of Canada
I learned in a one-roomed country school:

> *Louis Riel was a traitor;*
> *hanged in Regina*
> *for his treasonous acts*
> *as all traitors should be.*

> *Soldiers from Ontario came*
> *to rescue Saskatchewan*
> *from barbarity and bloodshed.*

Decisive and brief. No blurring
of right & wrong, black & white.

The accounts I memorized
were written and published
in distant Ontario. John A. MacDonald,
hero of the new dominion, built
the railroad that bore my ancestors
to their new wilderness homes
in the west. We didn't learn
John A. was a drunk, a procrastinator
who'd earn the dubious epithet,
"Old Tomorrow."

Canada's schoolbook history taught me
heroes had no flaws, traitors no virtues.
Movies were in black & white then, too.

So, what then *is* the true
history of this country? Are we
writing it at this moment, now,
as our feet scuff the path
between rectory and graveyard
perched on this height above
the broad bend of river?
Here, where Dumont's monument
oversees the river's slow turn,
where just over a century ago
he ordered cable slung below sight
across the swift spring flow,
then yanked the smokestack off
the steaming Northcote–
an inglorious end to the first
naval assault in our province's
limited battle chronicles. Who
will write the true history
of our land if not our poets?

Louis Riel was a poet.
So was D'Arcy McGee.
One was hanged, the other shot.
Poetry can be dangerous.

Al Purdy, once camped with his wife
on these same battlefields of Batoche,
claimed he heard voices in the grass,
though Eurithe, of much soberer disposition,
ascribed the voices to Purdy's penchant
for musing aloud and hearing only
those things he wished to hear.

We all try hard to listen and see:

the eyes encompass it with time—
bullet holes, rifle pits, grave sites,
Middleton's zareba, vantage points;
the ears in time discern sounds—
the westerly stirring the grasses,
turning poplar leaves, the sharp whistle
of ground squirrel, coarse crow chatter,
faint intrusion of a distant aircraft.

But it is *voices* we all want–
Purdy's voices or any others.
Each of us. This is what we
secretly desire: voices
that will speak to us
in a language that is
ours only.

I can not hear the voice
that may or may not whisper
in the ear of Doucet.
Nor can I hear the words
that may be falling softly
upon the ear of Lee.

                    *   *   *

She strode among the headstones as if on fire.
Margaret Laurence. 1977. An April day–
gloomy, cold, almost foreboding,
hardly spring-like. I walked beside her
for a time, here in this graveyard.
Sombre in heavy grey woollen cloak,
hood up to fend off the bite of wind,
she burned with a mission. I abandoned
any pretense of guiding, her passion
for this place she'd never seen
taking over entirely. She pursued some
inner zeal until she'd seen it all, had run
her fingers over stone and wood,
gravestones and crosses, had fixed
the rough texture of history forever
in her consciousness, making it hers
in a way that each of us must
make it ours, then give it
to our children and our grandchildren.

How long must we endure the raucous claptrap
of constitutional bombast and harangue,
the strident declarations of rights
without the faintest whisper
of accompanying responsibilities,
the endless negations of what
we are or want to be
or what we can become?

We need voices from Batoche
and Fish Creek, from Port Royal
and Brantford, from abandoned
outports in Newfoundland
and Haida villages lost to alders;
voices from the shut-down mines,
the dying prairie villages
and ghost fishing outports.

Instead of petulant songs
of differences, give us
singers of simple passion,
proud to give their children
a nation they can love.

History is the scorecard of victors.

But a century later, Batoche is
no longer just the place-name
for a quashed uprising.

> Riel,
>
> Dumont,

respectability gained in the grave.
The Metis people, uprooted
and dispersed by the economics
of exploitation, are returning.
Here at Batoche they reclaim their place.
Some day we may all know
what it was to be

> an expelled *Acadien*
> a dispossessed Metis.

Doucet has removed his shoes and socks.
Now barefoot in the grass, he grants

his toes the sensations his other senses
have experienced, lets them romp

in prairie wool, lets them store
their own memories in a part of him

he hopes he will later be able to tap
when his feet choose to remember.

Each toe must have something
separate and distinct to reveal:

minuscule traces of the thunder
of myriad bison hooves that shook

the rolling grasslands for days on end
a hundred fifty years ago?

faint vibrations of the wheel and whirl
of Cree ponies on the fringes of the herd?

Perhaps the grasses retain echoing shrieks,
the awesome cacophony of Metis carts

leaving their trademark wake on the grassy sea.
Can the toes sense this?

31

Or is Doucet simply saying to his feet:
Look, you've felt your way across

sandy beaches and rocky shorelines;
you've felt the maple and beech leaves

of eastern autumn woods; you've
crunched gravel and squeaked snow.

Now try this place
and tell me what you know.

We bear the unmeasured weight
of what we think we know—
also the more knowable weight
of our ignorance. Perhaps it is
just the being here, sharing
the soft scuffle of leather
and toes through the old stories
grass can tell—
our shared senses.

From this height of prairie grass
above the South Saskatchewan we look
south over the water's slow flow,
look towards distant Saskatoon.
If we are intent we can pick out the spire
of the old Metis church at Fish Creek.
Where we walk our feet may fall
into palpable depressions, rifle pits
dug by Middleton's or Dumont's men
more than a century past, vantage points
to command the surrounding terrain,
survey movements of all but ghosts.

We walk, imagine ourselves Metis hunters,
perhaps those raw recruits, shunted across
two thousand miles of wilderness
on a new railroad, then marched
over a fearsome plain to face
a faceless enemy, the first skirmish
at Fish Creek just upriver
from where we stand.

Faces to the warming sun and wind
we stand silent on our past,
looking toward some distant hope,
looking to find our place
in what this day has given us.

∞

The Dozer Man and the Owl

The Dozer Man and the Owl

Shaman

Baffin Island. Brilliant with summer,
flower bursts flood the brief season
and hillsides flaunt their colours
like spring-gladdened girls.

Sunday. Work at a rare standstill.
The dozer man on a day of rest
goes walking, wanders through
incredible hues of Arctic July,
intoxicated with landscape.
He tops a rise of land,
sees below him Inuit
gathered in a natural amphitheatre.

One man leads his people in ceremony.
The dozer man imagines it an invocation
of the sun. He can not be sure. So he
watches, remains at his vantage point,
sees the ritual through to its end.
He is silent. The shaman's incantations
evoke something he does not comprehend–
his desire to descend the hill, speak
with this man he has never seen.
He does not know the words he wants to say;
the shaman may not even share
a common language. The need
intensifies as he watches, as he listens.

Ceremony over, the dozer man moves
down the slope, moves like a dreamer
through his own dreamscape.
The Inuit disperse. Except for
the shaman who waits as though
this rendezvous were prearranged.
The dozer man seethes with questions,
imponderables that swirl and whine
like blackflies around his head.
He offers the other his name,
seeks words to lift the veil
of mystery covering his eyes.

The shaman raises his hand,
silences all questions. His eyes
grip the dozer man, stranger
who has come a thousand miles
and more to this chance encounter
here on a sunlit Arctic stage.
He holds his visitor mute, then speaks:

> *I can say only this to you*
> *and you must hear me well.*
> *You must kill your god.*
> *Only then can you be free.*

As if the question had been asked,
the shaman adds:

When the time comes, you will know.

The dozer man is befuddled,
his tongue a lump of soapstone,
his mouth a clamped vise. These words
hold no meaning; they are a puzzle.
He does not even know he is
not free. Has never considered it.
Questions uncork his tongue, words
bubble. The shaman silences him,
repeats his admonition, word for word.
Then turns and walks away.

Baffled and perplexed, the dozer man
is deserted. His eyes have become
those of a great snowy owl, his wonder
the colour of Arctic summer.

Pilot of Earth Moving

The dozer man raises his glass:
            whiskey tinkles ice.
His pencil line moustache twitches.

   I'm a dozer man, me. Twenty-eight years.

Pierre Lavelle. The dozer man.
What's in a name *is* important here:
Do not call this man *cat-skinner*.
Pierre is *dozer man.*

This man conducts a half-million dollar
symphony of computerized tractor power.

   There's nowhere in the North
   I haven't been, tanksalot.

Pilot of earth and rock in motion.
Such a man will not be called cat-skinner.

Tuktoyaktuk, Rankin, Inuvik, Resolute...
Me 'n' my dozer's been there, tanksalot.

He downs the whiskey, swirls the ice,
presses the glass against his ear as if
he could hear the tumbling chimes
of an Arctic stream. Pierre Lavelle,
pilot of earth moving, moving earth,
a man assured of his own place
on a spinning planet, sure that place
is firm as his dozer on a bed of granite.
Dozer man signals for another drink.

Whiskey

Dozer man loves his rye whiskey–
a bottle a day when he is south,
away from his tractor. None at all
when he works. Between moves
he drinks– some cheap motel,
a daily circuit through the bars
and a bottle for his room at night...

Pierre is eight when he discovers
his grandfather's whiskey secreted
in a dining room cupboard. A teaspoon first.
Then a tablespoon. Then a small glass.
Nurtured at eight, his love of whiskey
grows until Grandfather notices,
complains of evaporation. From time
to time he casts thoughtful eyes
on his resourceful grandson.

At thirteen Pierre leaves home.
Confesses his five-year whiskey thievery,
shrinks from expected wrath, is not prepared
for the smile. His grandfather,
amused by the brazen whiskey-thief,
places his hand on the young man's shoulder:

> *I can see for sure*
> *I don't have to worry*
> *about you, Pierre.*
> *You already know how*
> *to take care of yourself.*

Grandfather

Dozer man's history:
>   son of a Basque father,
>   Quebecois mother, born
>   in Cleveland, fatherless at two,
>   taken by his mother to Quebec,
>   house of his grandfather– home.
>   House of childhood.

His grandfather imbues Pierre
with family adages and homilies,
preaches the value of self-sufficiency:

>   *If you can't take care*
> > *of yourself*
>   *then you might as well*
> > *go hang yourself.*

In the woods of Quebec, Pierre
fells trees, a thirteen year-old
among the roughest lumberjacks.
His grandfather's words nourish him
from bush camp to bush camp,
from hand-saw and axe to the seat
of a bulldozer. Lying on his bunk
in the black spruce silence,
his grandfather's words resound in his head.

Now in his late forties, his grandfather
long dead, dozer man still hears
that voice. After thirty-five years
his grandfather is still the beacon–
the brilliant star that lights his way.
He wears with pride his many-coloured coat
of self-reliance, gift of his grandfather.
Wherever dozer man may go
his grandfather's hand rests on his shoulder.

Incident in Labrador

A good dozer man understands the power
at his fingertips, the hazards of control.
The inexperienced and inept must pay
for carelessness or bad judgment.

The young operator argued with Pierre,
insisted the latest dozers wouldn't overturn
as older ones were known to do,
their drivers crushed to lifeless pulp.

Don't talk crazy! Dozers are dozers.
You don't believe that, you're stupid!

The young man laughed, mocked Pierre.
Called him a mother hen. A worry wart.

You're stupid! All dozers are the same.
You make one mistake, you're dead.

In late afternoon the call came for a bulldozer.
Ore-truck in the ditch, nine miles from camp:
dozer man needed to haul the truck back
onto the road. The young man responded.

Hours later, an urgent call. *Come quick!*
The first dozer overturned at the scene.
No hurry then. He's dead. Pierre's reply.
He went out and started his dozer anyway.

In his mind the scene nine miles from camp
already etched in brutal detail. The statistics:
just twenty-five years old, a wife, two kids
in Montreal. Just another rookie operator

who would not listen, who would not respect
the power beneath his fingers. Not the first.
The quarrel with the young man still
tolled in his head like a village bell, echoed

like the owl's sad refrain. Outside Pierre
steeled himself to the cold, the reality:
overturned dozer, the young man
trapped beneath, the quick death.

The head lay in the snow, guillotined
by the sudden slash of metal canopy,
flung by the force of the execution
several yards away in a snow bank.

The bloodied head stared from the snow.
No self-confidence, just horror in the eyes.
I told you, dozers are dozers,
Pierre whispered to the silent head.

Meeting for Lunch

Northern Manitoba. Dozers gouge
a channel through rock and gravel,
a barely noticeable scar in the vast
Pre-Cambrian wilderness. Dozer man
stops for lunch, leaves his machine
idling in the channel, scrambles
the embankment, finds a spot to sit,
removed for a while from diesel fumes,
the constant roar and shudder,
the steady vibration that echoes
through the bones at night.

He pours hot tea from his thermos.
Waits. Remembers his lunch arrangement
with the new kid who works
the dozer down the channel.
Where Pierre sits they will share lunch.

Pierre lights a cigarette, sips the scald
of tea, listens for the sound– the dozer
clanking up the channel, this deep
uneven gash that twists between rivers.
He hears the dozer. Faint at first, then louder.
It grinds along the rock-strewn channel.
He can not see it beyond the curve,
but dozer man recognizes the sound
of the tractor's fastest gear.
The cat roars into sight and Pierre's cup
freezes at his lips. His heart lurches.
There is no driver.

He knows what has happened,
sees it unfold in his mind:
The kid stands at the controls,
peering up the channel to spot Pierre,
dozer careening along the rough trench.
A sudden lurch, the kid pitched off
onto the metal cleats. Entangled, crushed.
No time to cry out or cross himself.
Dozer man recognizes all this.

But he also knows it falls on him
to stop this runaway. Down the bank
he bolts, throws his dozer into low gear,
turns, faces the killer head-on,
raises his dozer-blade to meet
the rogue's own upthrust blade:
the impact will do the least damage—
costly machines now become
the consideration in his mind.
The mangled body up the channel
disappears in the unwanted challenge.

The driverless dozer clanks and squeals,
metal cleats rasp and shriek on stone.
Dozer man sees blood on the tracks,
a single forlorn leather glove flapping,
still hooked on a metal cleat.

The two dozers meet, steel on steel,
jousting metal bighorns. Blade
clangs blade, the shock shrills
through the conifers, rebounds
from rock ledges, sets ravens
to panicky flight, startles a black bear
into an unaccustomed gallop, echoes
miles across the cool northern autumn.

Dozer man, in lower gear, halts the renegade,
reduces it to spinning. He leaps
from his mount, stops the other's engine,
then his own. In the sudden silence,
he just sits on his mute dozer.

At last he clambers up the embankment
once again, pours a second cup of tea.
And waits. He knows what follows.

The battling dozers, heard for miles,
brings the project foreman jouncing
in the company four-wheel drive
to where Pierre sits. The foreman stares
down the channel at the scene: two dozers
locked like spent and soundless lovers.
His sudden ire would shake Pierre
like an old rag in the jaws of a dog.

What the hell stupid kind of game
are you playing
with company equipment?

Game? Tanks a lot.
You think this is game?
You come with me. I'll show
you what kind of game it is.

Pierre leads him down the embankment,
takes him a short walk up the trench.
Dozer man shows him. Shows him
what's left. The kid. Just eighteen.

Some game, eh?

Pierre must say this to the foreman's back,
doubled over as the other is, puking.
The foreman has no reply.

Dozer man's blade is replaced:
he is back on the job next day.
A new operator is found.
The foreman is gone for a week.

Last Wishes

The last time dozer man saw him
his grandfather was near death.
He beckoned Pierre close to his bedside,
clasped his grandson's hand in the fierce
grip of those who fear that final trip:

Pierre, don't you let them bury me
in a grave beside the road, you hear me?
I've hated that traffic all my life.
All that noise. I won't sleep there, Pierre.

Find me a quiet place in the graveyard.
As far from the road as you can get.
You promise me that now, Pierre.
All I want is a little peace and quiet.

When Pierre once again had to return
to another northern job, his grandfather
still fluttered on the edge of the body's
two worlds like a white owl winging
over endless fields of snow.

Dozer man missed his grandfather's funeral.

News from the south often creeps its way
into remote Arctic islands. His grandfather
had been buried a week when this news
reached Pierre Lavelle. He heard
the owl before the notice came.

At the first break in the job dozer man
flew south to Montreal, then went
back to the village of his grandfather.
At the home of his uncle, he reminded
him of his grandfather's desire, inquired
where the old man had been buried.

Never mind! Don't talk about such things!
It does no good to talk of these things.
He is a free man at last. It is enough,
The dead are dead. They need nothing.
What does it matter where the bones lie?

Dozer man moved his grandfather's grave.

The Owl

Christmas. Holiday time for dozer man.
Arctic islands a distant summer memory.

In the Quebec village of his grandfather
dozer man relaxes into nightly rounds–

homes of relatives, drink and talk, music
and song spin night into morning.

In the house of his grandfather, now
his mother's, the night of the party,

Pierre walks out into the cold night to piss,
moonlight splashing silver on snow.

He stands alone under a flash of stars.
Hears the owl hoot. Very close.

Dozer man peers up and there above
in a large sugar maple he sees it:

a large snowy owl. He knows this bird,
his Arctic years. Strange, he muses.

He grew up here, yet never saw such
an owl until his dozer took him north.

Has this owl followed him home?
Dozer man feels uneasiness slide

in his veins, disquiet creep in his marrow.
Then the shaman's words return·

When the time comes you will know.

Dozer man decides.
Back in the house he finds it:

his grandfather's .22 rifle.
When the owl falls at his shot

he feels exhilaration. He has
never killed an owl before.

Next day the villagers come,
one by one, to see the owl.

No one can recall such a bird.
Dozer man and the owl are

the story of the holiday season.
Dozer man at peace with himself.

Another Whiskey

Dozer man has finished
his stories, orders another rye.
His moustache twitches as he
lapses into silence. He drinks.
Whatever he is thinking now
he is not prepared to share.

Perhaps he hears the familiar
voice of his grandfather, feels
that man's hand upon his shoulder.
Perhaps he hears the shaman's
incantations echoing
along the multi-coloured hills
of Arctic summer.

∞

On The Edge
of My Brother's Grave

On the Edge
of My Brother's Grave

The phone call. 5 a.m.
Brittle voice, knife
slice of chill.

Early September,
a fall of yellow leaves,
the front yard birch
turning gaunt.

Her voice:
      my brother's wife
forty-five minutes
a widow.

Tell Mother
      she says.

No, my brother. This can not be.

Bright autumn morning–
a throng of plaintive geese
dragging dawn across the sky.
Not like this...

I spoke to you on the phone
not three short days ago.
Nothing in your voice
would bring us to this.
What did I miss?

Mother and I were to drive
to Edmonton to see you–
this very morning
now crashed down
upon us like a misfelled tree.

You were so pleased
we were coming.

We are not ready.

Remember:

We drove the sheet of ice, the highway home
that winter evening after work– home.
Two young women waited and wondered
why they did: there were others closer
        and more predictable.

Driving the black ice, the car finding its way
of its own accord, accustomed to the route;
me holding the steering wheel, but no more
in control than you, mixing rum and cokes
as we slid past ditched half tons
        and jack-knifed semis;

and you took the banjo out and we sang
while I watched the road skitter past,
trying to avoid the slightest wheel movement,
maintaining a foolish speed, believing utterly,
stupidly,
        in our infallibility;

and the police, suddenly there,
just over a rise, stopping cars,
the Mountie coming over,
one we both knew, glancing in, our drinks–
telling us to take it easy:

      wondering, as we resumed
our crazed pace, whether he meant the rum,
the road, our lives– never getting an answer,
but getting home to our women just the same,
late again,

      full of song and as always,

driving on ice.

*   *   *

Golds, russets and bronzes
of aspen and birch–
a hurrying of leaves
across the cold graveyard,
as if readying for winter.
A single leaf
at the edge of the fresh grave,
pauses, then drops.

The eighth of September.
Here in Fort Smith an arctic wind
undermines the paltriness
of the fleeing sun.

> *This was your place*
> *You made this land yours.*
> *This north you made*
> *your own.*

I do not know this land.
This part of you.

Slaveys, Dogribs, Chipewyans–
these Dene people you loved
and came here to teach–
What name do they
give to this month?

I am a stranger
in my brother's land.

The *facts*– as we know them:

the medical history a narrative
of doctors, drugs and hospitals,
a chronicle of hope and pain
punctuated with doubt and despair.

Eight years of heavy chemo.
Endless pillage of the body,
a drug war to delay the inevitable,
years tantalized by remission
and the flowering hope
blooming alongside fear,
eight years of chemical highs
beguiling the depression,
the knowing.

Facts. A thick dossier,
notes, perhaps a computer disk
in the Cross Cancer Institute.
Is it filed under your name?
Or simply coded
Hodgkins & complications,
filed with others?
Cancer stalked you
with unhurried patience,
but didn't get you.

            This data says nothing
            of the chemistry that binds
            the bone and blood of brothers.

Pneumonia took you. This is
what they say, what is
recorded in the hospital records.

You went to sleep at night
expecting to see us the next day,
full of high spirits and optimism.
During the early morning a nurse
checked on you– you were gone.

> *You weren't being treated*
> *for pneumonia.*

Three times the cathedral bell
tolls your name. This town
become your home, this place
I do not know, that is not mine.

Far from the country churchyard
where our parents lie, the land
of our reckless youth, lamenting
bell-sound rides the autumn air
with departing geese. Death knell.
Even the Slave River crashing
coldly by the town can
not mute this terrible toll.

Inside the cathedral two solemn priests,
a Catholic and an Anglican, share
final rites for a lapsed Lutheran.

An honour guard silent at your side—
a young Chipewyan, former student.
A Legionnaire, you are accorded
rites of the fallen, your comrades
silent and stiff at death's attention.

Only sibling, older brother, I am
drawn for the first time to this land
you claimed, that claims you now
forever. And me wanting
it to be otherwise, wanting to have
been here while you were alive,
to know these many strangers
who call you friend, who mourn
this part wrenched from me.

Wearing this too-tight tie of guilt.

Remember:

I was seven that time in Vancouver
and you were not yet five.
I remember little of the telegram—
just Mother, torn with grief,
her brother killed on Juno Beach
in the war that was for us
the source of endless games.
Neither of us knew our fallen uncle
and I could not fathom how
the death of someone so distant
could bring such sorrow.

Here at the edge of your grave
memories sting; their acid burns
the corners of my eyes like acrid smoke.
I watch pebbles scatter underfoot,
hear the thud of falling earth
like stone-hammers on my chest.

Two priests, different servants
of the same words– these words
that can never ease this pain.

"This man was my teacher."

"He was my colleague."

"He was my buddy."

"He was my husband."

"He was my father."

"He was my son."

This man was my brother.

Priests, what are your words
to stop this bleeding?

No words to bind the wound
and fill the emptiness?

I need them now.

Remember:

that night you danced, a joy-crazed Zorba,
on the roof of my car? I was not amused.
The moon a pale bird on your shoulder,
your dance some impromptu exorcism,
something neither of us mentioned again...

Christ, I was embarrassed. Angry.
But loved you for what you were,
some uncaged spirit I could never
set free in myself. Sometimes inside
this fortress of unsaid words I have
spent so much time building, I long
for that same moonstruck night,
that I might have climbed
atop the car to dance with you
beneath applauding stars.

Your last letter to Mother:

you, arriving in her birthing agony
four decades before, returning to her
in your last words on paper
written from the Cancer Ward.
Words of pain– but not of death.

    My mouth is all blistered inside
    and the pain is almost constantly with me.

That hand I know so well,
that script so like my own.
I read them and my own mouth
flames, unuttered words burn,
the tongue twists to escape.

    I have to freeze my mouth before
    I can drink my liquid meals.

I have this letter.
I have this pain.

I am beside your widow in the pew,
joint grief fused in silence. My hands
feel cold, the arm that would reach
to comfort her is dead. My body stiff,
unwieldy, my tongue a useless lump,
I am lost here. Lost in the mystery
of our blood...

Remember:

you were twelve, I was fifteen,
naked swimmers in the creek of our boyhood,
throwing the dog into the water,
running the length of our laughter
over grass, the dog furious in pursuit,
springing at you, its claws
ripping your thigh,
the crimson flow that bound
our careless youth and through
the later years of our separation,
the scar on your thigh, the memento
you would carry with you always–
the scar,
the blood...

What have I given you?
What have you given me?

What I am left with: memories.
just one survivor
left to sort and sift
whatever is left to me.

What have you taken from me?
What have I taken from you?

Voices of childhood
whisper down long nights
like dry leaves over gravel...

two boys, one is eight
and the other coming six, walking
along East Hastings in Burnaby,
pulling a wooden-sided wagon...

they have been to the fish market
where a nickel has bought
a treasure of fish heads,
redolent trimmings and scraps
for their fat grey tabby...

The voices faint, almost
unfamiliar, the language like
a lost ancestral tongue...

    they are happy and they are close:
    one hand each clasps the wagon's handle,
    flesh and bone on flesh and bone
    they pull their Saturday booty home,

    pull their wagon together towards
    some time beyond their knowing...

Your flag-draped casket,
maple leaf-blood of autumn,
this land dark with brooding
spruce and pine, stiff with mourning
against the waning yellow birch.

Six Legionnaires bear you here,
poppies stain their blue blazers.
They shoulder their memories,
step death's slow rite:
the flag, taken from the casket,
the ritual of folding, the four
corners of life bound together.

Poppies unpinned, each pall bearer
in turn steps forward to the grave,
stands above the casket, casts
his blood flower into your grave.

I can not look into the grave.

Each fold of the flag
is something lost,
each poppy bursts
inside me.

Remember:

that night we were returning home,
the weekend wild with wedding dancing?

Just the two of us, winding down at last.
We talked of the future, no looking back.

Now there is only looking back. No dances
to share. Just empty floors where once

we filled the night with laughter, and words
that whirled and swirled and spun around us

like promises of spring. How many dreams
we shared came true? Which ones did we lose?

It was June. Just three months before.
I drove to Edmonton to meet you
and we spent ourselves in talk over beer,
relived boyhood exploits, replayed
adolescent misadventures, laughed
with and at each other's faulty recall,
each certain of the integrity of his own.

*Did you know then how little time
was left to us to share as brothers?*

We shared so many dreams, spoke
of things begun, things undone.
This was to be the last sharing.
I can't believe you knew it then
and didn't tell me. Late at night
you spoke at length of your trial:
life lived within a crumbling body.

The morning came on too fast.
I fumbled for words that might
lift you from your pain, words
with wings to soar above
the terrible and utter loneliness
inside the failing body...

Words failed me then,
they fail me now.
What good unsaid words?

And now who is left
to tell your stories?

How you could set a table
to gales of laughter!

And who will choose,
now that you have gone,

that single word or phrase
that always found its mark?

You were your father's son,
much more glib than I who

labours on the empty page
to find that very measure

that you knew by blood...
On the edge of your grave

my tongue is frozen.

At the edge of your grave
a bitter wind warns
of winter. I am numb:
this unexpected severing,
bonds lost. The stony earth
has taken you.
I turn away, scuffle
the fallen leaves, move
away from this place,
the cold grave's edge,
away from you
and all that was.

∞